GENERATION GIRLS

Heartfelt advice, stories, poems and letters written by teenage girls for teenage girls.

Compiled by Tess Woods

Copyright © 2018 Author of each story.
Compiled by Tess Woods.

All rights reserved. No part of this book may be used or reproduced by any means, graphic, electronic, or mechanical, including photocopying, recording, taping or by any information storage retrieval system without the written permission of the copyright owner except in the case of brief quotations embodied in critical articles and reviews.

Because of the dynamic nature of the Internet, any web addresses or links contained in this book may have changed since publication and may no longer be valid.

The views expressed in this work are solely those of the authors and do not necessarily reflect the views of the publisher and the publisher hereby disclaims any responsibility for them.

National Library of Australia
Cataloguing-in-Publication data:
Generation Girls
ISBN: 978-0-6483116-4-5
Young adult, non-fiction, general.

Cover design by Thomas Paul Artistry

Publisher details: Karen Mc Dermott
www.karenmcdermott.com.au

DEDICATION

To all the girls out there who believe they can.

INTRODUCTION

Sharmila Nagar

Ballajura Community College is a large government school which caters for students from Year Seven to Year Twelve in the north-eastern suburbs of Perth. The college boasts many successes from academic to sporting prowess, and most importantly a team of dedicated educators and college staff. One of the many strengths of the college is that there are approximately sixty different languages spoken, providing a rich tapestry of culture. So, when Tess Woods volunteered to do a writing workshop with a small group of girls, it was extremely important to choose girls who would represent the college's diversity and also look at who would most benefit from the program. In the end, our intimate group of twelve girls (Years Nine-Ten) were chosen from various backgrounds, abilities and aptitude.

It was an absolute pleasure working with Tess Woods on this writing programme. The gentle way in which she encouraged the girls to write, think about challenging teenage issues and created a safe environment for them to experiment with different writing styles, was endearing and inspirational to observe. She truly brought out the best in every girl who was involved in the writing process.

Thank you to all the girls who participated in this programme, but thank you TESS without whom none of this would be possible.

Tess Woods

In 2017, I connected with an inspirational English teacher by the name of Sharmila Nagar from Ballajura Community College, a public school in Perth, Western Australia. Sharmila was open to my idea of a reading and creative writing programme to empower teen girls. Twelve motivated girls in middle school accepted the invitation to take part in the programme and we kicked off at the start of 2018.

My motives for starting the programme were to open a safe space for girls to engage in meaningful conversations about the issues that affect them, to encourage them to make good decisions, to help them make new friends and most of all to inspire them to discover the treasures within the pages of books and to create some of that magic themselves through their own writing.

For the reading component of the programme, we formed a book club. Each time we met, the girls chose one of the dozens of Young Adult novels that were donated from local bookshops. The girls read the books at home and then reviewed them for the others the next time we got together.

For the writing part, we covered topics that included relationships, consent, peer group pressure, social media, careers, high school legacies and the importance of seeking out happiness in the midst of difficulties. The girls blew me away with their candid, raw and heartfelt conversations. I loved the way they listened to, respected and supported each other.

The classroom we were in was called 'Purple Six'. We had a hard and fast rule: 'What happens in Purple Six stays in Purple Six.' In this way, the girls built a deep trust between one another. They had passionate powerful conversations where they shared heartbreaking stories and they also had hilarious conversations that had us in fits of laughter — there was never a dull moment!

After each session, the girls had a task to write a creative piece on the topic we'd discussed. They wrote everything from letters, to poems, to dark fairy tales, to interviews, to speeches. There were no rules, no word limits, no marks given. It was writing for the sake of expression and nothing more. In class, I taught the girls some creative writing skills. I critiqued each piece of work for them and then I watched in wonder as week after week they became stronger, more confident and skilled writers. Their pieces were touching, funny, sweet, chilling, achingly sad. You'll find samples of their creative writing work in the pages of this very special book. Some of the writing here will make you laugh, some might be confronting and some of it isn't for the faint of heart! Please be aware that the focus of our programme was on 'creative' writing so the girls have taken creative liberties with their stories, including those that are mostly autobiographical.

What I hoped when I first created this programme was that the skills the girls took away at the end of it would help them in school and in life - academically, spiritually and mentally. What I didn't expect was how deeply they would impact my own life and imprint on my heart.

These twelve girls haven't had it easy. They don't come from privilege and they have faced challenges that some adults would crumble under. Many of them have English as a second language so they had the extra hurdle of creative writing in a language that didn't come naturally to them. But they amazed me with their open hearts, their resilience, their eagerness to learn, their warmth and exuberance and their dedication to doing the extra work I pushed onto them.

I'm so incredibly proud of their creative writing pieces, which apart from spelling and grammar changes and the shortening of some passages, remain wholly unchanged with no editing. The girls had full creative expression with this book – from the cover photo concept to their name, 'Generation Girls', to the dedication at the front of the book, to the charity, Books in Homes, which they chose to donate 100% of profits to - this entire book is theirs and theirs alone.

Before you dive into this anthology, please allow me to acknowledge some key players in the Generation Girls project. Thank you Rebecca Sparrow for inspiring me to begin this project and backing it from the get-go. Thank you Sharmila Nagar for opening your heart and inviting me into your school. Thank you to the Ballajura Community College leadership team and the English Department for taking a risk with a new, untested programme. Thank you Karen McDermott for your generous soul in making this publishing dream come true. Thank you to my son, Thomas, for the beautiful cover design. Most of all thank you to the brilliant and inspiring Generation Girls. I hope the twelve of you continue to grow in self-belief, strength and kindness every day and may you inspire girls everywhere with the wonderful advice and stories you've shared here.

And finally, to the girls reading this – after you read these stories, go and write your own. You all have stories inside you that are worth telling. Believe in yourselves with great ferocity because the world is yours for the taking!

From Tess x

Inside each of us is a natural-born storyteller, waiting to be released.
ROBIN MOORE, AUTHOR

Meet the GENERATION GIRLS

ABI

Abi arrived in Australia as a shy ten-year-old girl from Jaffana, Sri Lanka. As a teen, she has a positive personality and a great character. She starts each new day with a smile and hopes to end it with an achievement or new knowledge. She never gives up and she keeps moving forward no matter what. She expects the unexpected and always tries to do the right thing.

Abi's hobbies include watching TV and reading manga. Since completing this program she has developed a love for writing and hopes to be a writer in the future or a scientist!

AN

An is the only girl in her Vietnamese family of boys. She is very passionate about her studies, so her family's move to Australia for her to get a better education meant the world to her. As soon as she arrived in Australia, everything changed and now she looks forward to a better life than she ever dreamed of before. An is a crazy K-pop fan, she especially loves GOT 7! Her other loves include reading romance novels and pampering herself by doing her nails and make-up.

CINDY

Cindy has been strongly influenced by her Vietnamese family and culture. She understands what other high school girls go through with pressures from school, family and friends because she is just the same. There are very high expectations put on Cindy so she tries hard to make herself and her family proud. When she isn't studying, she loves watching Korean dramas and listening to K-pop especially GOT 7. She hopes to one day be a successful businesswoman, who is strong, fearless and most importantly, independent.

FATIMA

Fatima is an independent and feisty Afghani-Australian feminist who has big dreams and a love of poetry and soccer. She might not be the best singer in the world but she still sings 24/7. Fatima loves exploring new things and hopes to travel to countries all around the world finding inspiration everywhere she goes. If you were to ask Fatima what she would want to be when she grows up, she would answer that she wants to be happy and to keep striving to become a better version of herself.

KAIJING

Kaijing's friends gave her the nickname Ka-ching which has stuck with her since Year Eight! She loves art and cooking. She's also pretty awesome at washing dishes and doing chores. Kaijing is particularly interested in manga and anime and she thinks some of the characters are totally handsome. Kaijing dreams of having a career in the arts. She isn't sure what exactly, but hopes it will incorporate her love of drawing and anime.

KIRA D

Kira D is an avid music lover. She grew up in Perth with her parents, brother and dog and she is part of a supportive and huge extended Italian family. Her family have supported her through her passions including singing and technology and now with her new-found passion for books and writing. As for the future, she hopes that somehow she can make the world a better place even if it is just lifting the spirits of another or helping fix a phone.

KIRA T

Kira T has aspired to be a YA author for most of her life and she loves to read. When she's not reading or working on her fictional worlds, Kira can be found sleeping, eating or begrudgingly being forced to do school work. She goes to unnecessary lengths to put meaning behind seemingly small things, like flowers and names but then finds she has no time to do homework. Kira enjoys belting out numbers from her favourite musicals and sleeping from four in the morning until midday.

NOORIA

Nooria is interested in art and craft and she loves creating cards and gifts for others. She also enjoys playing soccer and having fun with her friends. Nooria has a passion for learning new languages — she already speaks Hazaragi and English and has been teaching herself Hindi and Thai by watching Bollywood movies and Thai 'lakorns'. She believes in fairness and equality and that all people should be respected, whatever their religion or cultural background. Nooria is always caring of others, showing kindness and compassion to those around her. Her hope for the future is to work with those less fortunate than her, and to use her creative skills in some way.

SHAMILLA

Shamilla moved to Australia from Burundi hoping for a great future. She is independent and believes in miracles. She loves Maths and Art and hopes to become a lawyer one day. Shamilla's friends and cousins bring her happiness. She believes that everyone's beliefs should be respected.

TAHNYKA

Tahnyka has been through so much in her fifteen years and she has survived everything that Heaven and Earth have thrown at her. She doesn't let her circumstances hold her back and she keeps fighting every day. Tahnyka is the sort of person who mostly keeps her feelings about things to herself. She loves writing, anime, gaming, other countries and movies. To be continued…watch this space, readers, for more on Tahnyka in the future!

TASVEER

Tasveer is a fun and interesting character to be around. She's a comical, easy-going, responsible and reliable person. Her favourite subjects at school are Music, Science and English. She absolutely loves reading whenever she gets the chance. She also enjoys dancing, playing tennis, and playing instruments including the piano, drums, guitar and saxophone. Other passions include learning more about aerospace engineering, and digitally producing her own music.

YASMIN

Yasmin is as sweet as the jasmine flower that her name originates from but she is also confident, courageous and straightforward. She grew up in a mountainous region in Afghanistan and at the age of eight she immigrated to Australia with the help of her father. She has made some great friends who she hopes will be with her along life's journey. Yasmin's hobbies include reading, drawing, painting, singing and dancing to K-pop music. She enjoys playing sports, especially soccer. Yasmin hopes to be a great business woman or astronomer!

GENERATION GIRLS ON RELATIONSHIPS:

It's okay to walk away from a bad relationship. Even if it's hard and you think you can't, you will be okay if you walk away.

Don't let yourself love someone more than they love you.

Wait to have a boyfriend. Just wait until you're old enough to cope if you get hurt.

Don't change for anybody. Ever!

Love yourself more than you love anyone else. You're the most important one.

Just because he asks, doesn't mean you have to say yes.

Don't believe it if someone says you're ugly. You're just not!

If you're in a relationship where you can't share your problems,

then that's not a great relationship.

Everybody allows that the talent of writing agreeable letters is peculiarly female
JANE AUSTEN, AUTHOR

LETTERS

KIRA D

Just so you guys know, we're all in Year Nine or Ten, we're not professionals or anything. Just normal girls in high school. And here we are with a full blown book. We got this far and all we did were sessions in a writing club.

You don't have to be a professional, you don't have to be an expert to do amazing things. Honestly even as I'm writing this I'm amazed, I still can't believe that I'm actually going to be in a book with all these gorgeous girls.

Just because you aren't doing anything now doesn't mean that you can't do amazing things in the future, it doesn't mean you can't leave your legacy. You don't have to prove to the world that you can do great things. All you have to do is have faith in yourself and believe that you are amazing and you will be.

Even if you don't believe that, if you are in a tough spot in your life, just know that you'll get through this. If you don't think that anyone cares, that you can't get through it, then know this – I care, Generation Girls care. Everyone here, at this very writing club has had struggles too and we believe in you.

Because you *are* amazing.

You *can* do it.

Love from,

Me and all the authors.

ABI

Hello future me,

I'm writing to give you some advice. Right now I still don't know what I want to be - a cook, sports player, teacher, doctor? Who knows? Sometimes I think it would have been more exciting to live in times before there even were jobs – when humans had to hunt to eat and survive. Regular jobs seem dull compared to that. So If you end up doing a job you don't like, be brave and change it for something you love.

What makes life interesting for me now is that I don't know what you would have faced in the future. It's almost like you and I are in a marathon that we run and never stop until we die. Just remember, you have to keep moving forwards and not back down. If you stop, time won't stop for you. So be ready for anything and never ever give up. Don't think badly of yourself and don't forget to enjoy your life to the fullest. I'm doing that now!

I believe that everything is here for a reason and everything has positives and negatives. Think of both good and bad sides when faced with problems. Also remember that no problem is too big to be solved, there is a way through everything.

Be thankful for what you have and what everyone does for you. Keep doing the right thing and don't lose track of the right path. Believe in yourself and find new heights to keep reaching out for. Keep loving yourself no matter what.

Although you are older than me, I just don't want you to forget these things. Please give us a happy future that we can both enjoy.

Love from your teenage self, Abi.

KIRA T

Dear Dad,

It's been five years since you and Mum died in the car accident and still not a day goes by that I don't think about the two of you. I live with Grandpa now, I used to live with Grandma until she died six months ago from ovarian cancer. We released her ashes in the same place we released yours, under the cherry blossom tree in the Zen park. But I guess you already know all that, you live here (for lack of a better term). Anyway, I'm here to tell you about how I've been doing. My birthday was last week, I turned fifteen! It's okay if you didn't remember, you're dead, I wouldn't expect you to.

Grandpa and I had a picnic under your tree, he said he could feel you all there. You and Grandma, Mum, Nana and Pop. I didn't really feel anything but I went along with it for him. I don't visit the tree often but Grandpa does. He comes here every Sunday. He used to go to church as I'm sure you'll remember, but he just doesn't have the spirit anymore, so he sits on the bench beneath your tree instead and weeps. I fear Grandpa may not be well; he was never the same after the car accident and, since Grandma passed away, he's been so distant. I don't know how to make him feel better. I don't know how to help.

The doctors say that we can only hope that whoever killed you and Mum is caught, that maybe getting that closure will help him with his grief.

By now, the police have realised that the crash was no accident, someone cut the brakes to harm you. They still haven't caught the person who sabotaged the car five years ago. They keep saying they're closer than they were at the beginning. They're grasping at straws.

I miss you so much, I hope you're doing better in death than you did in life.

Your Waterlily.

PS I'm sorry for cutting the brakes.

YASMIN

Dear future me,

I'm Yasmin, your teenage self. I'm writing to let you know that I have wishes and dreams for my future that are really important to me and I want you to achieve them!

Firstly, I want you to be independent. I'm independent already, but not that much yet because I still have Mum and Dad by my side. It would mean a lot to me for you to experience living alone and supporting yourself with your own money. So I want you to work hard and earn that money without anyone's help.

Secondly I really want you to go to university. I know it's my job to study right now and I promise that I am studying but sometimes I also need a break. If you remember the school breaks aren't that long!

I hope you remember your years in high school, from the worst parts to the best parts. And I really hope you at least try to forget the painful memories and instead think about the special times you had there.

So yeah, that's about all I wanted to tell you!

Yours,

Yasmin.

TAHNYKA

Dear twenty-year-old me,

    I hope you've been growing and learning and *living*. I also hope that you've made a new life for yourself now and that you're happy with how it's going. I hope to the goddess of love and caring that you passed Year Twelve. I don't expect you to have your dream job or a serious partner just yet, but I do hope you're having fun. And I also hope you've got friends around you that you love and trust.

    Love from your fifteen-year-old self who has lots of hope in her heart that all of this will come true!

    Nyk.

CINDY

Dear Chau,

I'm Cindy, your future teenage self, writing to you to let you know that there are tonnes of things I want to say to you and want you to change and do. Also there are things that I wish you hadn't done.

For example, don't give up acrobatics, keep going. Why, you ask? Because when you stop you won't do any other exercise and you'll be so unfit and unhealthy. So don't quit even though it hurts and your body aches after every lesson.

I know right now you are feeling confused, you feel like you don't belong there and happen to be different from people around you. I know you think your homeroom teacher hates you. You also feel lonely because you don't have a truly close friend to express yourself to so you're always keeping everything in. I know you feel pressured and stuck because Mum and Dad have very high expectations of you and at the same time, you also feel ashamed of yourself. Your body (short and overweight) and your skin colour (dark) are different from people around you and this gets you down. I also know that you have to study hard and prepare for your Year Five end of year exam which determines what kind of secondary school you'll be going to next year. You feel stressed and you think you might fail the exam. (You will fail by the way.)

The main reason I want to write this letter is to tell you that everything is going to be fine, you will eventually get over all of those things and finally be happy. I know you're now asking yourself, 'How can I feel happy now that you've told me I'm going to fail my exam?'

So I'm here to tell you that you're going to leave Vietnam and fly to Australia very soon, so the exam mark doesn't really matter. You're going to have a new name, a new life and start all over again. In Perth, you'll find friends and teachers who love you and who accept your skin tone and body shape without humiliating you.

If you want to learn guitar – do it! If you want to start doing martial arts — do it! If you want to do anything, just do it and enjoy it. Don't be scared to start a new thing because you might miss out on a very good opportunity and then you'll be sitting here as Cindy in a few years and you'll be asking yourself why didn't you do those things when you had the chance.

Love from your future self,

Cindy.

GENERATION GIRLS ON SOCIAL MEDIA

Wait until you're thirteen before you sign up.

If you feel like you can't tell your mum what you're doing on there, then you are probably doing something you shouldn't be.

Take responsibility for what you say.

Keep your settings to private.

If you are always connected on social media, you are probably disconnected from your actual life.

Live as much as you can in your real life instead of an on-line life.

Always have a friend you know in real life connected in group chats with friends you only know online.

Set yourself daily boundaries for how long you'll spend on it and stick to them.

Skype or FaceTime the people you meet online so you know who you are actually speaking to.

Try not to get addicted to seeing who likes or comments on your stuff and setting those expectations for your friends. As long as they are good to you in real life, don't rely on their online activity to base your friendship on.

The true poem
rests between the words
VANNA BONTA, AUTHOR

POETRY

AN

What is youth?

It's about being a rebel

It's an endless story

The laughter of happiness

It's about the memories

Those moments that you waste without even noticing

That's youth

That special time of your life

The time where you meet your seven 'I's'

I am glorious

I am beautiful

I am strong

I am risky

I am vulnerable

I am sad

And finally

I am blooming

That's youth

But…

Without you realising it

It's gone

Once it's passed

It will never come back

So embrace every moment of your youth

Because youth

Only comes once

KAIJING

What are Memories?

We all have memories that are harsh,

Having a hard time does not mean it's the end.

Life's adventure simply takes time,

Tears are important.

Inside of me is strength

I am endless like the sky.

Memories begin with an encounter,

But relationships can go on after mistakes.

An end means there's a fresh start,

School is only the beginning of our memories.

FATIMA

Her Childhood Legacy

She was a combination of wild and innocent.

Just like the moon, she could light up the whole world just with her smile.

She dreamed of living in a peaceful world, away from terrorism.

She lived by her moral code and left her kindness and cheeky smile as her legacy when she said good bye to her childhood and stepped into a teenage world.

A world where there were humans but not humanity,

A world where teens didn't play with toys anymore, they played with phones and people's hearts instead.

The world she stepped into changed the way she viewed things, but not her beliefs.

Despite living in an inhumane world, she still believed that there were pure hearts filled with love hid behind those dark masks.

In this unknown world, full of lost people, she started a journey to find her inner self.

Years passed…

Her independence grew,

Where there was innocence there now lived knowledge.

She lived and learnt what living actually means.

She learnt that sometimes life isn't fair. Life is a test.

She learnt that it was up to her to be fair, not life.

Her teen problems were worth it because they made her the person she is today.

NOORIA

Just Because

Just because I am quiet,

Doesn't mean I will always be quiet,

Doesn't mean I can't raise my voice,

Doesn't mean I don't care,

I can raise my voice for my rights and I will.

Just because I am a girl,

Doesn't mean I am not as good as men,

Doesn't mean I am just a housewife,

Doesn't mean I can't hang out with boys,

I am a girl and I want freedom.

Just because I am Muslim,

Doesn't mean I am a terrorist,

Doesn't mean I hate other religions,

Doesn't mean I take people's lives,

I am Muslim and I want freedom.

TAHNYKA

Like a Sister

Your hair is as red as fire,

But your eyes are as cold as ice.

You're as sweet as sugar,

But I'm not that nice.

You are the yin to my yang,

The light to my darkness.

You are the burger to my fries,

And that's why I love you so.

But I don't understand why you

Stay and why you don't let go.

You are the coolest person I know and I'm not,

And that's why I love you so.

KIRA D

Sticks and Stones

They hurt, the sticks and stones

Sometimes I wish no one would notice

The scars they're stitched and sewn

Yet they don't centre their attention.

Sticks and stones will break my bones but words will never hurt me

The words repeat in my head

And I must agree to these words of hope

Yet I fret at the feeling of dread.

Sticks and stone will break my bones but words will never hurt me

Come on, come on they have to be real

It can't be, they can't lie to me

Though the words they said seem to be true.

The cage around my fragile heart

It's cracked, shattered

I try to repair what once was whole

Though nothing works, the creases still show.

Just because sticks and stones don't break my bones

It does not mean

That words cannot break me inside.

TASVEER

Free Rein

The night fell

And out rang the town's bell

The animals grieved in the moonlight

Its striking glow made the night bright.

Two broken souls laden with a baby

All alone, motherless and unsteady

Gypsies they were called: travellers of invaded land

Searching for life second-hand.

Clang! Clang! The metal bars screamed

Displaying the deserted animals as a team

Fear and misery echoed through the zoo

Losing Alice and the zookeeper was painful too.

Hopes of release like candle light

Hopes of finding the keys shone bright

The candle burned out long before

The animals and children could reach for more.

A ladylike figure rose from the ashes

Shaded by the greyness of dawn's flashes

Freedom in death she stood for

Release of pain she called for.

SHAMILLA

Life is a Ladder

Saying goodbye to my past now,

Never looking back, focusing on my destination and the right people will come after my arrival.

People come and go,

Others pass by and touch my soul.

Some teach both positive and negative lessons.

Life is my road, some will walk with me but they can't walk it for me,

All these people play a role in my life,

They'll break me down or make me complete.

These people fill my day and night.

To those who played a role in my journey, I am truly grateful.

CINDY

Best Friends

Every one of them is awesome

And special in their own way

But somehow crazy at the same time.

The things they say and do are so crazy that only I could understand them.

Friends, I will always fight for you,

Respect you and be right next to you when you need.

I will always include you,

Encouraging you every step of life.

And I will

Never

Turn my back on you.

So, Best Friends

Don't you dare lose me.

GENERATION GIRLS ON HOW TO FIND HAPPINESS IN TOUGH TIMES

1. Put on upbeat music
2. Pat your pets
3. Learn to sew and make something
4. Colour in
5. Be yourself. If you aren't pretending to be someone you're not then you will be happier
6. Try something new
7. Read
8. Remember that in the end, everything is okay
9. Exercise
10. Meditate
11. Spend time with friends
12. Do something that requires concentration like shooting hoops or Sudoku
13. Look up at the stars
14. See a sunset
15. Have a good cry and let it all out
16. Go for a walk
17. Have a cup of tea with a sprinkle of cinnamon
18. Write in a journal
19. Watch a favourite movie
20. Bake something yummy and eat it
21. Or don't bake but just eat yummy food!
22. Try and focus on the good stuff instead of the bad stuff

There's always room for a story
that can transport people
JK ROWLING, AUTHOR

LIGHT TALES, DARK TALES, MEMOIRS AND MORE

KIRA T

The Girl Who Loved Death.

Once, there was a girl.

The girl loved Death more than anything else. She loved Him more than all the stars in the sky, she loved Him more than the dying cats in the streets, she loved Him more than a king loved his queen. She was drawn to Him much like a moth was drawn to a flame, but the girl was sad, for Death did not love her back. For years, she tried to seduce Him, but to no avail. The girl simply wished to spend her time with Death, for He protected her from the monster.

You see the girl, strong as she was, had only one weakness; the monster that haunted her every waking moment. Life. The girl feared Life, she hated Her but she never seemed to be able to escape Her clutches. Many around her told her that she was lucky, that Life was good and that she should embrace Her but this was not true for the girl.

For her, Life was all but happy, it was pain and suffering. Life was, to her at least, the same as Death was to others. And so, the girl hid from Life, locked in her room, talking to others just like her; others that lived thousands of miles away.

By her sixteenth year, however, the girl had grown tired of hiding. The monster living inside of her was too much. Life whispered cruel nothings within her mind as she gripped a knife, the point hovering above her heart. The girl could no longer stay away from the One she loved.

Her eyes lowered to the blade, her breath heavy, her body weightless.

'O happy dagger, this is thy sheath. There rust and let me die.'

The blade was cool, contrasting with the heat of the girl's final breaths. Dark shadows danced within her vision and her mind. And as the shadows danced, she saw that being free from Life did not make her free. You see, Death has a way of clearing your mind of confusion. Only within the last moments of your existence do you realise things that should have been obvious from the very beginning.

So as the girl lay dying on a bed of stone stained by scarlet, she finally realised something that she should have figured out a long time ago. The girl did not love Death, she simply hadn't given Life a chance to be her friend.

SHAMILLA

My First Day in Australia

Everything was different. The weather was five times hotter than it was in Zambia.

My uncle and some of our family friends came to pick us up at the airport — it was very nice finally meeting relatives that I had only known through phone calls before then. They took us to the house that the government had prepared for us to stay in until we settled into our new lives. We all quickly showered and then we went to my uncle's house where the main celebration of our arrival was happening.

At that house, there were different types of drinks and snacks. While my parents talked about everything we had been through and the other grown-ups told them about what life was like in Australia, my cousin took me on a tour of her house. It was very clean — whatever I touched it didn't even have any dust on it!

My aunty and uncle took my older sister to buy phones for our family. My cousin and I joined them and walked around the shops ourselves. I couldn't believe how different the shopping centre was to our life in Zambia. Over there we lived in a refugee camp where we never had as much food. We bought heaps of treats. It was heaven!

When we headed back to the house, we watched a movie while munching on our snacks and it felt amazing. After the movie, we had to go home and get some sleep because we had a long day coming up the next day, we were going to be introduced to all the Burundian people my uncle knew.

It was great coming to Australia and I went to bed that night looking forward to my next day here!

ABI

The Princess and the Witch

In a faraway land, further than the long river, further than the beautiful forest which was home to many animals and further than the witch's hut, was a beautiful kingdom. Ruled by the fair ruler, King Ozwhith and his kind and beautiful wife, Queen Soamea, the kingdom was the best it had ever been.

But it wasn't perfect.

The queen had not become a mother yet and she and the kingdom were in deep sorrow.

After many years, the queen joyfully became pregnant and Princess Seropherina was born. Seropherina was known to be a very beautiful yet different princess. She didn't cry like the other babies or make it hard for the maids to clean her.

One sunny day, no different than any other, the queen picked up her baby girl and took her out into the royal garden. It was the queen's first time going out with her daughter and the princess was fascinated by the beauty of the garden. The princess smiled and suddenly light at the speed of lightning shot from the princess's hand to the queen's tiara turning it into chocolate. That was when the whole kingdom came to know that their princess wasn't ordinary. She was magical.

Not so far away from the kingdom lived a witch whose name was Maorna. She had a dark heart that was filled with greed for power. She killed anything and everything that stood in her way. One night she rode on her broom to the forest to collect the ingredients for her potion. On the same night, two personal guards of the king were walking nearby. The guards were talking about Princess Seropherina and her magical powers of turning the queen's tiara into chocolate. When Maorna heard this, she put her invisibility cloak on and went straight to the castle on a mission to steal Princess Seropherina's power from her.

Seropherina was in deep sleep when Maorna found her. The wicked witch reached out to touch Seropherina but the princess had a protective barrier surrounding her with her mother's love. Despite the love shield around Seropherina, Maorna still managed to use her dark magic to lift the baby princess into the air.

Terrified, Princess Seropherina started crying and everyone in the castle came running.

Since Maorna was invisible, nobody knew she was there but they wondered why the princess was floating in the air. They just assumed it was another kind of Seropherina's magic. Laughing her evil cackle, the witch took the crying princess back to her hut. Nobody went after them because they thought the floating princess would return.

But the queen recognised that evil laugh. It was the same laugh that Quortient used to have, who happened to be the witch's mother. The queen ran to her room and took out her magical globe.

She used it to connect to the witch's mother and then she questioned her. 'Quortient what have you done?'

'My queen, what are you talking about?' said Quortient. 'What happened?'

'You have somehow stolen my daughter and I want her back!'

Just then, Maorna flew into their witch's hut with Seropherina.

Without a word, Quortient quickly put a spell on Maorna that turned her into a baby who was identical to the princess. She put the princess in a basket and her daughter in another basket and sent them both floating across the river but in different directions. The witch floated in the direction of the castle, while the princess floated in the opposite direction.

Maorna, who was now in the form of the baby princess, understood what Quortient's plan was. Her mother, who was even more evil than she was, had worked out an even better plan to destroy the kingdom.

When the baby witch was found floating near the castle, there was a note attached to her basket.

My dearest queen, I am so sorry for my daughter's doing. I have banished her forever and your daughter is no longer in danger. Here is your child, I am giving her back to you.

Maorna was joyfully received by the castle guards and the true princess had floated to somewhere far far away, never to be seen again.

CINDY

A Speech

Teachers, parents, friends and fellow students, it is an honour for me to speak to all of you today. To be honest, I'm freaking out a little right now because I used to be a person who was scared of talking to people, so to be up here in front of this large group of you is a huge step for me. About five years ago, I moved to Australia and started school here. At first, I had no idea what everyone was talking to me about or when they were trying to tell me to do something. I could only understand if anyone asked me my name and that was it. I couldn't even understand when a teacher ask me one simple question, 'Do you have anything to write with?' I just stared at her and kept saying, 'I don't know'.

But here I am today, standing in front of all of you giving a speech *in English*. Five years have passed and many things have changed. I now can understand, write and *speak* fluent English! And I'm still working hard on building my confidence.

Back in Vietnam I used to be an overweight girl with skin colour that the people there considered " ugly". This made me feel horrible about myself and I even hated myself. I didn't have any close friends because I was too shy to approach anyone. I would sit alone in the library staring at groups of friends that sat together. It was in those moments that I would repeat one thing to myself that made me feel even worse, 'It's because you're ugly,that they don't want to be friends with you.' I tried to fit in by losing my weight but I just wasn't happy.

However, when I moved to Australia, I learned to open up more as I met many people from different parts of the world and, just like me, they were also "different". I made the decision to do things to give myself confidence. I forced myself to learn to play music because this was a way to make myself stand up in front of groups, people and perform. This definitely helped me feel more confident about myself and my body. I fetl happy and, for the first time, I felt like I fitted in. As a person who once had low self-esteem, I was inspired by a quote from a book called *365 Days of Wonders*. The quote was, 'You were born an original, don't become a copy.' So now when I talk to myself, instead of saying, 'You're ugly,' I say, 'You're different, but that just means that you're special and unique.'

So, friends, I am here today to tell you to be confident about yourself because nobody is perfect. Embrace yourself! Every morning wake up, look into the mirror and say to yourself, 'I am special and unique.' Leave all the bad stuff behind and go do all the things you want to do, don't be afraid to try anything — do it all now and then you won't have regrets later. You only live once. Carpe Diem! Seize the day!

AN

Don't Judge a Book by its Cover

'Good morning, sir. How can I help you today?' Hailey, the receptionist kindly asked.

'Hi, my mum needs false teeth because she's been struggling lately,' Jackson, the young man who was accompanying an older lady, replied.

'Just wait a minute, I'll be right back.' Hailey gave him a smile and disappeared into the office. She came back a minute later with a booklet filled with photos of different types of dentures along with the cost of each set. The prices ranged from the cheapest to the most expensive dentures.

Jackson took a quick look over the booklet then he gave it to his mum. 'Mum, choose the ones that you want,' he gently said.

His mum, Sophia, looked over the booklet very carefully a few times and then she finally pointed to a set of dentures. 'Excuse me,' she told Hailey. 'I want this one please.'

'Are you sure you want this one, madam?' Hailey asked. 'This is the cheapest set so it isn't very good quality. It might be uncomfortable when you're eating.'

'I don't mind. I like this one, so please do it for me,' Sophia answered.

Before Hailey took any further action, she looked to Jackson to see if he would have anything to say about this.

'Just do whatever my mum told you,' Jackson said with an unsmiling face.

'Okay sure,' Hailey answered. 'Sir, before we go ahead, we need you to do some paper work for us, and pay first.'

'Okay.' Jackson stood up and walked towards Hailey.

He filled in the forms and gave them back to her.

When it came to the payment, Hailey thought that Jackson was going to pay but she was wrong. Sophia paid for herself. The cash that Sophia pulled out of her wallet wasn't big notes but it was a pile of small notes and cents that she counted out on the reception desk.

Hailey felt very sorry for Sophia. Her son had driven a Mercedes into the dentist's car park, he was wearing clothes from all the top fashion brands around the world and he even had on gold jewellery.

But his mum had to pay this bill for herself. With an old mum who could die at any time, how could her son treat her like that? Even though she was very angry, Hailey needed to be nice because they were the customers. She sadly took the money from Sophia.

'Thank you, madam. Now, please follow me.' She turned to Jackson. 'Sir, you can just sit here and wait for your mum, please. It won't take very long.'

After taking Sophia to the treatment room, Hailey knocked on the dentist's office door. 'Daniel, there's a patient waiting for her teeth to be fixed.' She told Daniel about what had happened in the reception area.

Daniel was upset to hear the story. 'Hailey, please bring in the most expensive set of dentures and take the amount that is owing out of my wages this week. I cannot believe that there are still people like her son in this world who are so selfish.'

There was a knock at the door..

'Come in.' Daniel turned his head to the door.

'Oh, sorry to interrupt. Can I speak to you, please?' Jackson asked Daniel.

Daniel gave Jackson a cold look. 'Yes? How can I help you?'

Jackson pulled out a pile of cash from his wallet.

'Can you please give my mum the best set of dentures? She's worked hard all her life for me to have the best things. I want to always respect her so when she decided on the cheap dentures, I didn't want to go against her decision in front of her because I always obey her. But I also want to do everything that I can do for her so she can be happy. I want to pay back all her hard work, even if she doesn't know I'm paying all her bills like this one. So can you please try your best? I want the end result to be perfect. Thank you.' Jackson gave Daniel the money and walked outside, leaving Daniel behind with all his thoughts giving him a headache.

Hailey was having the same thoughts as Daniel. 'Geez, I judged that person wrongly. I shouldn't have judged him because I didn't know the story behind him as a person.'

Hailey and Daniel were both very regretful in that the moment.

After that day, both Hailey and Daniel tried their best not to judge people without knowing more about them first. And they took very good care of Sophia.

KAIJING

Journal entry

21/3/2018

Thursday

Weather — Cold

If anyone asked me what is the hardest thing to maintain in the world, I would say relationships with people. Relationships are so hard. Even a little argument can lead to a relationship breakdown.

For me, a good relationship is maintained by forgiving and apologising. Almost everything can be solved by having a respectful talk. Why would some people rather argue than have a calm talk? There are ways to keep relationships strong. For example, better relationships with parents can be built by spending time with them every week. Relationships with friends can be strengthened by simply hanging out with them at recess, lunch and, after school, by texting or calling them. Relationships with your boyfriend or girlfriend can be made stronger by accepting their opinions and ideas.

Sometimes I feel like I don't want to maintain a relationship anymore because I'm too tired, and relationships take effort. Sometimes I want to give up, but in my mind there's a voice telling me that if I give up then everything that I've had before with that person would disappear. The only things that would be left are memories. And then eventually even your memories would fade and you would become nothing to each other except for people who entered each other's worlds, as if by accident, and then walked away.

From what I have experienced before, I don't want this to happen again, because every time it happens, I become a little more scarred inside.

So my wish is that I can maintain the relationships I have now. I think that I have good relationships with people that I care about, and the people who care about me. I don't need many relationships, but those that I have I want to keep until the day that I get so old, I can't even talk anymore.

KIRA D

Best Friends and Heroes

'Damian, this could totally work! Can't you see it?' Rosette swung her pale legs and jumped off the counter top. 'The Desert Rose. Newest Hero to New York City.'

Damian raised an eyebrow. '*The Desert Rose*? Since when was that a thing?' He leaned back in his black swivel chair.

'It's my hero name! I came up with it last night.' She grinned widely, bouncing on the balls of her feet. 'What do you think of it?'

He sighed, turning back to his desk, where pieces of scattered paper lay. Rummaging around the paper, he pulled a blank sheet. 'Well if that's your hero name, we'll need to make you a hero costume to fit that name. I'm thinking, green, black and red. Those are the main colours.' While Damian spoke, he sketched a basic outline.

Rose squealed. 'Yes, I love it!'

A short while later the outfit was ready for Rose to try on.

Damian's mouth fell agape at the sight of her. 'Who are you and what have you done with my best friend?'

Rose laughed, fidgeting with the hem of her forest green mini skirt. 'Yes, I know it's a shock, but I, the Desert Rose, am your best friend, Rosette!'

He shook his head. 'You look amazing and I knew that mask was a good call.'

Rose took off the black mask that covered her eyes. Varying sizes of small thorned green stems ran along her outfit, ending with gorgeous red roses, ranging between fully blown flowers and small buds. She wore black trainers with bright green laces.

Damian rolled his eyes. 'Now, "Desert Rose', he used air quotes around her hero name as he turned in his chair, rolling over to his computer across the room. 'All we have left to do is wait for something to happen that needs a hero.'

'New York always has something going on,' she replied.

****

Four months later, as Rosette had foretold, something did happen.

Rosette leapt from building to building along the neon lit rooftops of New York City.

She looked down at the mass destruction below, people screaming as they desperately avoided falling pieces of debris. Gritting her teeth at the sight, she turned away to take a deep, calming breath. 'You can do this, Rose.'

Suddenly, her breathing halted. Realisation hit her hard — she wasn't the superhero she wanted to be. She was just a human, an ordinary human. She was the same as the civilians, scared and alone. 'I could n-never do this,' a small whimper escaped her lips. Her legs were shaking before her knees gave way and she collapsed on the roof of the building.

'*Rosette*!' Harshly, she was pulled from her thoughts as Damian's voice came out from the walkie-talkie attached to her hip.

'Yeah?'

'What's wrong with you? I can see you're frozen up there! These people need you out there!'

'I'm sorry, Damian, I can't do this.'

'What do you mean, you can't do this? The Rosette I know wouldn't give up so easily, the Rosette I know wanted to be a hero, a Desert Rose!' he yelled.

His words gave her the strength to push herself off the rough rooftop. She stumbled on her shaky legs before finally regaining her balance. 'Thank you, Damian.'

Finally, she scaled her way down the building to where the chaos was.

She stood on a destroyed car, attempting to gain the attention of the crowd. 'I know how scary this must be but we need to stay calm!' she yelled. 'Look! There's an exit out of here where police officers are waiting!'

She hopped off the car to help people towards the safe zone before she was shoved harshly to the ground by a frantic lady, running in the opposite direction.

She dusted herself off as she stood, putting a hand on the lady's shoulder. 'Ma'am, it's not safe here.'

The lady turned around with wide eyes, tears running down her face. 'M-my daughter! I can't-can't find her!' Delving into her purse, she pulled out a small picture of a little girl.

Rosette skimmed over the picture. 'I'll find her, just please go to safety!' Not waiting for a response, she raced to find the child. Feet pounding on the black, ash-ridden road, weaving in and out of cars and dodging debris. Looking high and low, under cars and fallen chunks of the crumbling building.

She heard a whimper coming from her left.

'Mummy, help! I-I scared!' A small girl was curled up between a car and a large broken piece of bricked wall.

'Hey, hey. It's okay. I can take you to your mummy,' Rosette cooed as she crouched down to the girl's height, her hand outstretched towards her.

The little girl hesitantly let Rosette take her hand. Rosette quickly pulled her up into her arms and rushed towards the exit. Her lungs felt about ready to burst, her legs felt like jelly and her breath came out in shallow puffs of air.

She was so close when something went wrong. A piece of debris fell right in front of her and she wasn't able to stop in time. She tumbled to the ground, twisting her body to protect the child. 'I promise you'll be okay,' she assured her.

Then it happened, it was as if it was in slow motion. The crumbling building landed straight on her. The only thing she could hear was the cracking of bones, the ripping of her own flesh and finally the screams of the little girl beneath her. Yet she held herself up on her forearms, keeping the little girl safe as the world descended into black.

****

Slowly, Rosette's eyes fluttered open. 'Where-where am I?' she croaked in a raspy voice..

Damien took her into his arms. 'I knew it! I knew you'd wake up!'

'What happened? Where am I? Who are you?'

'I-I'm your best friend, Damian.'

She examined his face. 'Who-who am I?'

Damian bit his lip. ' You're Rosette Overly, you're twenty-four-years old and you're a hero. You have a heart of gold, you're funny, sassy, caring, intelligent, the list could go on forever. You-you didn't have a family, we were all we had since we were in the orphanage together as small children. You always wanted to help people, to be the hero even though you were just a normal person. If only I had let you know, that you were always a hero to me.'

Imagining Rose was still alive could only go on for so long before he had to face the truth.

He squeezed his eyes shut. If only it was a dream.

He turned, not ready to face the cruel world by himself. Into the almost empty car park he shuffled, stumbling every so often before reaching his black car.

Taking one last glance over his shoulder, he whispered his final parting words to her. 'Goodbye, Rosette.'

KIRA T

The Seasons

      Summer is beachy. She walks around with tanned skin, blonde waves and piercing purple eyes, dressed in a flowy, off-shoulder blouse, acid-washed shorts and a handmade seashell crown. She has a bright personality and a smile that could outshine the sun. She always has sand stuck to some part of her body and wears bright bikinis that can be seen beneath her blouse. She likes surfing.

      Autumn wears auburn colours. He has bright green eyes that contrast his brown-red hair. No matter the time of year he always seems to wear a scarf around his neck and sometimes a beanie. He ties his hair in a small ponytail in the back to stop it from blowing around his face at the lightest wind. Autumn is an artist, when not painting he can be found nursing his pet squirrels, Hazel and October. He loves pumpkin pie and the sound of dry leaves crunching beneath his feet.

      Winter comes across as a cold person, but he sometimes struggles to hide his warm heart. He can't stand heat and has commitment issues (just like me). That's not to say that he can't stay committed to one girl, he's just terrified of the very idea, he's never even tried it. Winter has black hair and piercing blue eyes. He loves hot chocolate and coffee that warms him during the cold season. Though he insists otherwise, Winter secretly loves Autumn's pets Hazel and October. He is the oldest.

      Spring is the youngest of the group. She cuts her hair short every winter, growing it out for the remainder of the year. Spring has a knack for nature photography, with her soft amber eyes can find beauty others would overlook. When she's not rescuing stray animals or taking photographs of the surrounding nature, Spring enjoys sunbathing in the meadows. Last year, she made a daisy crown for Winter, to everyone's surprise he wore it (as well as a practised scowl) and he refused to take it off until the flowers wilted and fell from his hair (warm heart, like I said). Ironically, Spring has severe allergies.

TASVEER

Cold Case

The blade pierced through the ice, as a flowing silhouette glided across the arena, leaving the whole crowd on edge. Her elegant dress and skilful turns pleased the judges greatly. As her confidence filled her mind, she felt a surge of daring. Summoning all her strength, she launched herself into the air. Then there was a loud thud as she landed hard, sliding across the ice. Her eyes blurred, as she felt herself being lifted from the cold miserable ground. She was a disappointment to her team, especially her father, the coach.

****

'Sierra, it's time to wake up,' a motherly voice spoke gently.

She moved her body out of bed, but immediately collapsed back down. Her head still pounded hard, and her legs were all bruised up. As far as she could remember, she was about to perform a triple lutz, her favourite and most reliable move, until everything went black. But how? She trusted her routine greatly, she was bound to win the annual Australian Figure Skating Contest with her glorious routine. She was the best in her team after all.

Later that day her mother urged her to go to support her dear friends and team mates at practice. In Sierra's mind this was not possible. How could she face all her team mates after her embarrassing fall and how could she look her father in the eye? He had always supported her, and he had even sold his much loved motorbike, in order to pay for the expenses that this competition required.

However, eventually Sierra found herself limping down the stairs to a compact ice-rink that her father had rented for practice sessions.

There were her friends, in what seemed to be new uniforms. They walked past Sierra with unforgiving glares. Even her closest friend ignored her as she walked past with the team. For some reason, one teammate in particular, Rowland, grabbed Sierra's attention. Rowland seemed more confident than usual. After all Sierra was quite intimidating, as she was able to do almost anything with her skates on. However, the looks that Rowland gave Sierra were taunting. Something was up, and Sierra needed to get to the bottom of it quickly.

Quietly, Sierra followed Rowland who went with Sierra's best friend, Cindy, to the equipment room. What were they up to?

'Finally, she's out of the competition for good. Now we don't have to deal with putting up with that boaster. Nice work, Rowland, she really did smash that performance!' Laughter erupted in the room as Cindy grinned at Rowland, holding Sierra's skates in one hand with the bolts in the other hand.

Sierra limped away, not believing what was so obvious. Her teammates sabotaged her. She had to tell her father.

After she told him, her father dismissed the class except for the three of them. He took a long deep breath and spoke to Rowland and Cindy. 'Sierra tells me that you both may have purposely unscrewed the bolts from her skates, to ruin her performance last night at the arena. Is that true?'

Rowland's face turned bright red. 'Sorry, I don't exactly understand what you are saying. We would never…' As Rowland was about to finish her sentence Cindy interrupted by saying, 'Sir, it's true, we did unscrew the bolts from her skates, but we didn't expect her to get badly injured.' Cindy pointed towards Sierra's bruised knees.

'We thought that if we unscrewed it she would trip, and get a bad score, and at last, it would give one of us a chance to finally take the spotlight from her. Every award we win is from Sierra, and I guess we were just really jealous,.'

However, an apology was not enough to persuade the coach to keep them on the team.

Several weeks passed and Sierra was back on the ice, knowing that her two least favourite people were out of her team, and that her fall was not her fault. She was better than ever. Though, she was humbled by the fact that her ex-best friend was jealous of her, she was also hurt that she was ultimately betrayed by her. Sierra hoped that she could compete in the contest again next year, especially without any embarrassing accidents to deal with again.

NOORIA

My Afghanistan

Glossary (in the order the words appear in the story)

Chishma — A large natural stream of water flowing in a channel

Abay — Mother

Tala — An open natural space field

Chukri — Payment

Gawra — A wooden cradle

Chori or karra — Traditional bangles

Baitulkhala — Toilet

Maktab — School

Bacha-posh — When a girl dresses up as a boy in Afghanistan. It is a cultural practice in which some families pick their daughters to dress and behave as a boy if they don't have a son.

Running through the mountains, herding sheep and milking cows were the best things about living in Afghanistan. We had loads of sheep, cows and hens. My uncles and aunts herded them every day early in the morning on the high mountains of Jaghuri. We used to bath in the *chishma* every day even if it was freezing. In winter we used to make snowmen and dress them with our own clothes. Before I was born, Abay used to take the cows to *tala* and climb to the high and sacred mountains of Almitu and Jaghuri to collect *chukri* for the family.

    I'm thankful to Abay for bringing me into the world, but I was not born at a good time for our family. When I was in Abay's womb, my grandmother passed away. It was the worst thing that ever happened to Abay and it was hard for her to choose whether to smile at my birth or cry at my grandmother's death. When I was small, it was like I could sense Abay's sorrows and I would cry continuously. Abay soothed me the only way she knew how, by singing a Hazaragi lullaby. *"Lullai lullai baache ma, ay noor e tu dide ma…"* But I still had trouble sleeping because of the sound of shaking the wooden *gawra*. And the strips of cloth that I was tied with were so tight and it made me feel like a mouse in a trap. Most Afghanis swaddle their babies with long strips of hand-made cloth to prevent them from falling over and to protect them from any dangers.

I remember my aunts chatting away as they washed the dirty dishes in the *chishma* close to our house, while the men used to make *chori* or *karra* or any other type of jewellery, or sometimes they used to tile walls. I want to go back to those moments when I used to laugh and play freely without any worries and tension.

My uncle and my older sister used to go to *chishma* together to wash their vehicle, I wanted to go too but I was too young. The chances of getting bitten by a wild dog were very high, even going to the *baitulkhala* at night was dangerous and the wolves could bite you, because it was very far from our house.

Our suffering and hardship began when the Taliban invaded our space. The Taliban whipped people in public so that the villagers would get scared and not go against them. Even if we followed their rules, we knew they could still kill us. When I was little, I always wanted to know if I would ever escape the Taliban because they killed so many for no reason. This was not the Islam I knew. It must have been even harder for my parents to keep living in such a place, where in the *chishma* blood was flowing instead of water.

The Taliban wanted boys to be more educated than girls and they expected the boys to grow up and be like them. Girls were not allowed to go to *maktab*, we were only allowed to stay home and learn how to be housewives. Parents did *bacha-posh* to their daughters. They dressed them as boys so that they could work and earn money for the family. The bacha-posh girls they used to do minor jobs such as, selling water, or wiping shoes. I can hardly wait for the day when Afghanistan will be a safe and peaceful country, when the Taliban will disappear forever and when girls and women can get justice.

Me on the right with my younger sister, Rana, when I was 10 years old in Islamabad.

www.ingramcontent.com/pod-product-compliance
Lightning Source LLC
Chambersburg PA
CBHW061814290426
44110CB00026B/2872